Parasaurolophus

Written by David White
Illustrated by Pam Mara
Cover Illustration ©
The Natural History Museum, London/Orbis
Project Edited by John R. Hutchinson

John Hutchinson is a graduate student at the University of California in Berkeley. He studies the anatomy and physics of dinosaur movement, as well as the evolution of dinosaurs. In particular he has worked on how large dinosaurs such as Tyrannosaurus rex might have stood, walked, or even ran.

Library of Congress Cataloging in Publication Data

White, David, 1952–July 13–
    Parasaurolophus / David White.
        p. cm.–(Dinosaur library)
    ISBN 1-58952-031-9
        1. Parasaurolophus–Juvenile literature.
        [1. Parasaurolophus. 2. Dinosaurs]I. Mara, Pamela, ill.
        II. Title. III. Series.

QE862.065W452   2001   00066534
567.914—dc21

Printed in the USA

Rourke Publishing LLC
Vero Beach, FL 32964

Quetzalcoatlus

Parasaurolophus

Deinosuchus

Corythosaurus

Spinosaurus

Oviraptor

Parasaurolophus

Pachycephalosaurus

Anatosaurus

Struthiomimus

Euoplocephalus

Rutiodon

Psittacosaurus

Parasaurolophus woke as the first rays of the sun broke into the glade. The grass was heavy with dew and a mist hung over the lake. Around her, the herd was stirring. She could see their crests through the mist as they lifted their heads to sniff the morning air.

The strong scent of the sequoias drew them to their feet. They were hungry. Calmly, yet purposefully, they made their way to the edge of the pine forest and began to feed on the upper branches. Soon the woods were full of the sounds of their grunting as they chewed on the pine needles and called to each other through the trees.

Parasaurolophus did not go with them. Instead she set off toward the lake. There she found what she was looking for: a long low mound of earth with an opening at one end. This was the nest that she had built for her young. She had made it by stripping the branches from a tree and covering them with mud.

A large snake lay curled on top of the nest. He was waiting patiently for the young to emerge. Parasaurolophus drove him away with a quick movement of her head. She pushed her snout into the entrance of the nest and snorted. Soon, the head of the first of her young appeared. He had to squeeze his body through the entrance, since he was now as large as many full grown dinosaurs.

Ten more young followed him from the nest. Immediately, they headed for the water. Soon they were swimming strongly quite a way out in the lake. Now and then they would plunge their heads into the water, searching for soft weeds to eat. Their teeth were not yet strong enough to chew the tough needles of the pine trees.

Parasaurolophus kept watch as they swam and fed. She knew that there was danger in the reeds that grew at the water's edge. The reeds hid the huge Deinosuchus, who would snap up any creature who came too near.

Further along the lakeside, Parasaurolophus could see the crests of a herd of Corythosaurus that had come down from the forest to drink. Their young playfully splashed in the shallows. Suddenly there was a roar and a rush of water. Deinosuchus launched himself at one of the Corythosaurus. For a moment his mighty jaws could be seen as they gripped the neck of the animal. Then both disappeared into the reeds.

Parasaurolophus remained at the water's edge with her young. She knew that they were safe. Deinosuchus had found the food he needed and would not threaten them for a while.

When they had eaten enough, Parasaurolophus signaled to her young, with a series of grunts, that it was time to leave the lake. She then led them back to the nest. The sun was high in the sky. It was time for her to feed.

Parasaurolophus went to join the rest of the herd at the forest's edge. Soon she was browsing on the branches of a plane tree. Suddenly, the sound of eating stopped. The herd scented danger. Parasaurolophus turned to look across the open land. Her keen eyes soon spotted the danger. Gorgosaurus was approaching.

Parasaurolophus and the rest of the herd broke away from the trees and hurried toward the lake. The water was their refuge. They knew that Gorgosaurus could not pursue them there.

First they had to reach the water. As Parasaurolophus lumbered toward the lake, she could sense that Gorgosaurus was gaining on them.

At last they reached the lake. Eagerly, Parasaurolophus plunged in with the rest of the herd and swam strongly away from the shore, propelled by powerful strokes of her great tail.

Gorgosaurus halted at the side of the lake. He could follow no further. Cheated of his prey, he turned and loped back up the slope toward the plain.

The danger past, Parasaurolophus swam back to the shore. She returned to the nest to see if all was well. She found the nest undisturbed and her young safe inside.

When the young ones heard Parasaurolophus arrive, they knew it was safe to leave the nest. Outside they fought mock battles while Parasaurolophus dozed in the heat of the afternoon. Struthiomimus sprinted by in her restless search for food. She paused near Parasaurolophus and parted the grass with eager hands. She was looking for lizards and insects.

Suddenly, the peace of the lakeside was shattered. Two Triceratops were locked in combat. Parasaurolophus was unafraid. Triceratops would often fight among themselves, as one tried to show that he was stronger than another. However, they were no threat to her or her young.

The contest between the Triceratops ended as quickly as it had started. The winner snorted in triumph. The loser, who lost a horn in combat, retreated into the undergrowth.

The sun began to set, and the shadow cast by the nest mound grew longer. The young returned to the nest for the night. Parasaurolophus went to rejoin the herd at the forest's edge. She had not gone far before she heard the noise of scraping. She turned around. There, silhouetted in the setting sun, stood Dromaeosaurus. With his great claws he was hacking at the roof of the nest and tearing it open to reveal the frightened young inside.

Parasaurolophus knew she was no match for Dromaeosaurus. All she could do was to act as a decoy, to draw Dromaeosaurus away from the nest. Bravely, she ran toward him, snorting and grunting. Dromaeosaurus paused in his digging and turned toward her. He seemed undecided as to what to do.

Parasaurolophus pretended to run away. This encouraged Dromaeosaurus to give chase. Parasaurolophus desperately dodged this way and that in an attempt to escape. Dromaeosaurus soon caught up with her. He slashed at her with his claw, opening up a great wound in her back.

As Dromaeosaurus prepared to move in for the kill, he heard a roar of anger. It was Gorgosaurus, who had been attracted to the smell of blood. Gorgosaurus had not eaten for days and he was getting hungry. Believing that Parasaurolophus was his prey, he launched himself angrily at Dromaeosaurus.

Parasaurolophus saw her chance, and escaped into the woods. There she lay and licked the blood from her back. The wound would heal. Now, under the cover of night, she was safe.

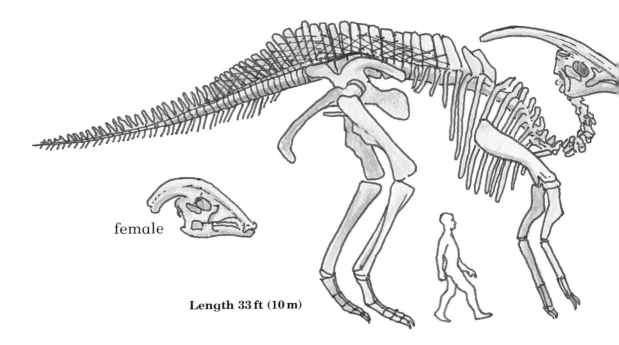

female

Length 33 ft (10 m)

The skeleton of Parasaurolophus compared in size with a man.

Parasaurolophus and Late Cretaceous Montana

The Time of Parasaurolophus

Geologists divide the Mesozoic Era, the "Age of the Dinosaurs," into three periods: the Triassic, the Jurassic and the Cretaceous. The Triassic lasted from 225 million to 195 million years ago, the Jurassic from 195 million to 136 million years ago and the Cretaceous – the longest period of them all – from 136 to 65 million years ago. This period was named after the great beds of chalk which were laid down at the time ("creta" is Latin for "chalk"). Parasaurolophus lived in the latter part of the Cretaceous, often known as the Upper Cretaceous, some 80 million years ago.

The Land of Parasaurolophus

In the Late Cretaceous, the continents started to take the shape they have today. While seas flooded Europe, they receded from North and South America, which became joined for the first time. The land was much flatter than it is today, with a vast inland sea extending from the Gulf of Mexico to the Hudson Bay. The great mountain chains of the Rockies and the Andes had not yet been thrust up by movements of the Earth's crust. However, much of the landscape would be familiar to us today, with many trees, flowers and birds that we would recognize. The story takes place in what is now Montana, an area which was thickly populated with dinosaurs. We know this because the fossilized remains of every order and suborder have been found in the sandstone rocks.

The Family Tree of Parasaurolophus

Parasaurolophus was a hadrosaur, or duck-billed dinosaur. Hadrosaurs were probably the most successful of all dinosaurs. They were descended from the bird-hipped Ornithopods. The earliest hadrosaur, Protohadros, lived in Texas in the early Upper Cretaceous period. By the end of the Cretaceous, hadrosaurs were established in Europe and Asia. The greatest number, however, were found in North America, where they evolved into many different types. Three main groups developed: the flat-headed, the solid-crested and the hollow-crested. Parasaurolophus, perhaps the most remarkable looking of all, belonged to the hollow-crested group. There have been many arguments about the purpose of the strange crests. Scientists think that the extended nasal passages inside the crests may have given them an acute sense of smell enabling them to sense danger and increasing their awareness of each other.

Other plant eaters

Herbivores far outnumbered carnivores in this period. Ornithopods (bird-hipped) became more numerous and varied. There were three main groups of plant eaters in the Late Cretaceous: the hadrosaurs, the ankylosaurs (the armored dinosaurs) and the ceratopsians (the horned or frilled dinosaurs). Triceratops, who appears in our story, was one of the most successful ceratopsians and survived in large numbers right to the end of the Cretaceous.

Meat eaters

In the Cretaceous period, the plant eaters fed on the forests and the flesh eaters fed on the plant eaters. Carnivorous dinosaurs had an important function keeping the numbers of plant eaters down and preventing the overgrazing of the forests. The late Cretaceous was the heyday of the carnivorous dinosaurs. There were two main types: the mighty tyrannosaurs and the generally smaller but faster coelurosaurs. Tyrannosaurus and Gorgosaurus were notable examples of tyrannosaurs while Deinonychus and Struthiomimus were very different examples of coelurosaurs.

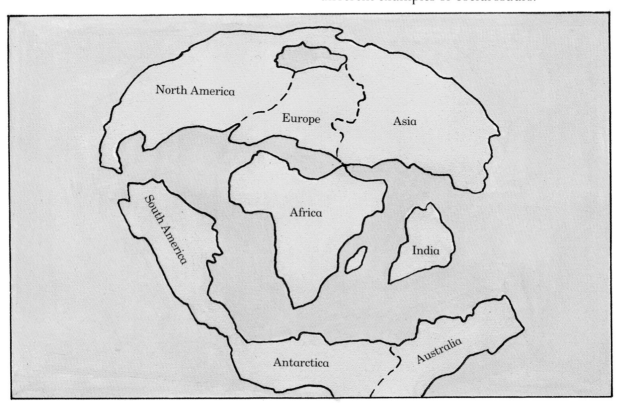

Map of the Cretaceous World